First Facts®

Transportation Zone

Tractors

in Action

by Peter Brady

CAPSTONE PRESS
a capstone imprint

First Facts is published by Capstone Press,
1710 Roe Crest Drive, North Mankato, Minnesota 56003.
www.capstonepub.com

 Books published by Capstone Press are manufactured with paper
containing at least 10 percent post-consumer waste.

Library of Congress Cataloging-in-Publication Data
Brady, Peter, 1944–
  Tractors in action / by Peter Brady.
      p. cm.— (First facts. Transportation zone)
  Includes bibliographical references and index.
  Summary: "Discusses the history, function, and workings of tractors"—Provided by
publisher.
  ISBN 978-1-4296-7693-9 (library binding)
  ISBN 978-1-4296-7969-5 (paperback)
  1. Farm tractors--Juvenile literature. I. Title.
  TL233.15B735 2012
  631.3'72—dc23   2011021525

Editorial Credits
Christine Peterson, editor; Sarah Bennett and Lori Bye, designers; Eric Gohl,
      media researcher; Kathy McColley, production specialist

Image Credits
Capstone Studio/Karon Dubke, 1, 8, 9, 11, 19, 21, 22
Getty Images/Hulton Archive, 17; Roger Viollet, 15
Shutterstock/Chas, 7; dusko, 4; Maksud, cover; NanoStock, 12

Printed in the United States of America in North Mankato, Minnesota.

102011   006405CGS12

Table of Contents

Tractors at Work

An engine hums as it helps pull a plow up and down a field. Huge tires move slowly through rows of growing crops. Farmers rely on tractors to get work done. Other operators use tractors to haul huge loads. These big-wheeled machines pull heavy equipment. They can move logs or clear snow.

Who Uses Tractors?

Farmers grow crops that feed people and **livestock**. Tractors make this work easier. Farmers use tractors to plant crops. Tractors also help farmers **tend** and harvest crops.

Other people use tractors to move snow or dirt. Large tractors pull trailers that carry rocks, logs, and other heavy loads. People use small tractors to mow lawns.

livestock: animals raised on a farm or ranch
tend: to look after or care for something

Parts of a Tractor

The driver gets a good view from the tractor's cab. The cab's glass sides allow the driver to see all around the tractor. The driver controls the tractor with a steering wheel and brakes.

duals

A powerful engine moves the tractor through a field. Huge tires have deep grooves called lugs. Lugs help keep tractors from getting stuck. **Duals** give some tractors even more grip.

dual: a pair of tires on each side of a tractor

How a Tractor Works

Tractors pull or push different types of attachments. Attachments plow fields, mow grass, bale hay, and carry heavy loads. A drawbar connects attachments to the tractor. A **power-takeoff** (PTO) runs the attachments. The PTO gets its power from a tractor's engine. A **hydraulic system** raises and lowers attachments.

hydraulic system

power-takeoff

power-takeoff: a unit attached to a tractor that provides power for other machines
hydraulic system: a system of pumps powered by fluid

disc harrow

Attachments

Tractor attachments help farmers do different jobs. Mowers cut hay and straw. Swath turners flip hay and straw so they can dry. Balers wrap dried hay and straw into bales. Planters put seeds into the ground. Cultivators dig up weeds that grow between rows of crops. Disc harrows chop soil and old crops.

13

Before Tractors

Before tractors, farmers relied on livestock to help get work done. Horses and oxen dragged wooden plows through hard ground. Farmers pushed the plows as they walked behind the animals. Farmers planted most crops by hand. Later, horse-drawn planters made this job easier.

Early Tractors

Farmers first used tractors in the 1870s. Steam engines powered these large machines. The first tractors had enough power to pull up to 40 plows. But these machines were too big for farm work. Farmers soon began using smaller tractors with engines that ran on gas or **kerosene**. These tractors were low to the ground. They couldn't pull machines through crops easily.

kerosene: a thin, colorless fuel that is made from petroleum

Tractors Today

Modern tractors combine speed and power. Diesel or gasoline engines power most tractors. Today's tractors have either two-wheel or four-wheel drive. Drivers control tractors more easily with power steering and power brakes. Rollover protection systems and seat belts help keep drivers safe.

Tractor Facts

- Tractors are heavy vehicles. Large, four-wheeled tractors can weigh up to 60,000 pounds (27,000 kilograms).

- Crawler tractors move on tracks like army tanks. The tracks form a loop around the tractor's wheels.

- Tractors are slow vehicles. The top speed for most tractors is 25 miles (40 kilometers) per hour. Because they move slowly, tractors are often driven on the side of the road.

- Large tractor attachments can weigh more than 5,000 pounds (2,260 kg).

Tractor engines do not use much fuel. A farmer keeps track of an engine's hours rather than its miles.

Hands On: Plant Your Own Crops

Do a tractor's work by planting a mini bean field. Tend the seeds and watch them grow!

What You Need

13 x 9 disposable aluminum baking pan
potting soil
plastic fork

10 bean seeds
water

What You Do

1. Fill a disposable aluminum baking pan with 6 inches (15 centimeters) of potting soil.
2. Use a plastic fork to form two long rows. The fork acts like a plow and breaks up the soil.
   The rows should be about 4 inches (10 cm) apart.
3. In each row, plant four bean seeds about 3 inches (7.6 cm) apart.
4. Cover the seeds with 0.5 inches (1.3 cm) of soil.
5. Gently water your field until the soil is moist.
6. Put the pan where it will get plenty of sunlight. Water the plants as needed.
7. Seeds will sprout in five to seven days.

Glossary

drawbar (DRAW-bahr)—a heavy bar attached to the back of a tractor that is used for pulling machinery such as a plow or mower

dual (DOO-uhl)—a pair of tires mounted to each side of a tractor or other machine

hydraulic system (hye-DRAW-lik SISS-tuhm)—a system of pumps powered by fluid forced through chambers or pipes

kerosene (KER-uh-seen)—a thin, colorless fuel that is made from petroleum

livestock (LIVE-stok)—animals, such as horses, sheep, and cows, that are raised on a farm or ranch

power-takeoff (POU-ur-TAYK-awf)—the part of a tractor that provides power for other machines

tend (TEND)—to look after or care for something

Read More

Dayton, Connor. *Tractors*. Farm Machines. New York: PowerKids Press, 2012.

Gregory, Josh. *Tractor*. What Does It Do? Ann Arbor, Mich.: Cherry Lake Pub., 2011.

Internet Sites

FactHound offers a safe, fun way to find Internet sites related to this book. All of the sites on FactHound have been researched by our staff.

Here's all you do:

Visit *www.facthound.com*

Type in this code: 9781429676939

 **Super-cool stuff!** Check out projects, games and lots more at **www.capstonekids.com**

Index